Food Industry Guide to Good Hygiene Practice

Mail Order Food

Regulation (EC) No. 852/2004 on the Hygiene of Foodstuffs
and
The temperature control requirements of the Food Hygiene
(England/Scotland/Wales/Northern Ireland) Regulations 2006

Published by TSO (The Stationery Office) and available from:

Online
www.tsoshop.co.uk

Mail, Telephone, Fax & E-mail
TSO
PO Box 29, Norwich, NR3 1GN
Telephone orders/General enquiries: 0870 600 5522
Fax orders: 0870 600 5533
E-mail: customer.services@tso.co.uk
Textphone 0870 240 3701

TSO Shops
123 Kingsway, London,WC2B 6PQ
020 7242 6393 Fax 020 7242 6394
16 Arthur Street, Belfast BT1 4GD
028 9023 8451 Fax 028 9023 5401
71 Lothian Road, Edinburgh EH3 9AZ
0870 606 5566 Fax 0870 606 5588

TSO@Blackwell and other Accredited Agents

ISBN   978-0-11-243097-1

First impression 2007

Foreword

Dame Deirdre Hutton CBE – Chair, Food Standards Agency

This *Industry Guide* provides food business operators with practical guidance on how to comply with general food hygiene legislation and related requirements. It has been officially recognised by the UK Food Standards Agency (FSA) and agreed with enforcers, industry and other relevant stakeholders.

The use of this guidance is optional and food business operators can choose to comply in other ways. However, where a food business operator is following the guidance in a recognised *Industry Guide*, the enforcement authority must take this into account when assessing compliance with the legislation. I believe that the use of such *Industry Guides* supports the proportionate, consistent and effective application of food hygiene legislation in the UK, which is why the FSA fully supports their development.

Contents

Part 1
Introduction

This booklet is a guide, for food businesses operating by mail order, on compliance with Regulation (EC) No. 852/2004 on the Hygiene of Foodstuffs and the temperature control requirements of the Food Hygiene (England/Scotland/Wales/ Northern Ireland) Regulations 2006. It is an official guide to the regulations and has been developed in accordance with Article 7 of the EU Regulation. Its preparation has followed the "Guidelines for the development of national voluntary guides to good hygiene practice" issued by the Food Standards Agency (2005). The guide has the status implied by Article 10.2(d) of EC Regulation 882/2004. Whilst this guide is not legally binding, officers from food authorities must "take it into account" when assessing compliance with the regulations.

The use of this guide by businesses is voluntary. However, it is hoped that the information in it will help you both to meet your legal obligations and to ensure food safety.

The guide deals only with the regulations quoted above, hence it refers only to issues of food hygiene and safety. Many other Acts of Parliament and Regulations impinge on the operation of mail order businesses, some of which will have a relevance to general food hygiene issues.

Part 2
Acknowledgements

The guide has been developed by the following group of stakeholders:

Name	Representing
Peter Austin	Mail Order Fine Foods Association
Paul Brown	Royal Mail
Chris Dabner	National Association of Master Bakers
Nick Read	British Trout Association
Ian Dent	Packaging Federation
David Lock	LACORS – Local Authorities Coordinators of Regulatory Services
Tom Miller OBE (Chairman)	Consultant*
Mike Ross-Browne	Mail Order Fine Foods Association
Marcus Themans	National Farmers Union

Assisted by the following observers representing the Food Standards Agency:

Name	Representing
Sarah Appleby	Imported Foods Division
Rob Griffin	Enforcement Division
Peter Midgley	FSA Scotland
Kevin Woodfine	Primary Production Division
Michelle Bayliss	Primary Production Division

* Engaged to produce this guide on behalf of the specific industry sector.

Part 3
Scope

This guide covers the sale of perishable foods by mail order, when delivery to the final consumer is in an unrefrigerated vehicle. The term "mail order" is used throughout to include all distance-selling operations, irrespective of how orders are received, e.g. by post, telephone, fax, email, internet, etc.

"Perishable foods" are defined in this context as those that are required by law, for food safety reasons, to be kept chilled/refrigerated and marked with a *use by* date when prepacked for retail display. See Appendix A for guidance on the likely products involved.

The guide's contents assume that the food, whether produced on site or bought in, is already within its primary wrapper* when it is first delivered to the mail order operation or mail order part of a larger food business. It is assumed there will be no handling of the food other than in its wrapping and no further preparation will take place before dispatch. This guide is limited to the mail order food part of a business operation and is not intended to cover all aspects of how the rest of the food business can comply with food hygiene and temperature control legislation. However, for completeness, Appendices C and D set out the full requirements of the legislation for information.

The relationship between the production/ manufacture of the food and the mail order distribution service can vary significantly. Sometimes the manufacturer of the product will sell it by mail order. On another occasion the seller may have no direct involvement in the food's production. For this reason, it would be inappropriate to provide food safety guidance to the producer/manufacturer or general distributor of food products in this mail order guide. There is a range of existing official *Industry Guides* that provide guidance to compliance and advice on good practice in respect of the hygiene and temperature control legislation. Thus they could be of general assistance to mail order operators

also. If no particular guide matches your business, the Wholesale Distributors Guide could be the most applicable.

This guide does not cover:

- foods delivered hot (e.g. pizzas, takeaway meals etc.) as they are for immediate consumption and delivery is generally over a relatively short time
- doorstep deliveries of supermarket groceries because of the short delivery time and distance.

It applies to the whole of the UK and to sales to addresses both within and outside the UK, whether within the European Union or not.

---

* *The EU Regulation defines "wrapping" as the placing of a foodstuff in a wrapper or container in direct contact with the foodstuff concerned, and the wrapper or container itself; and "packaging" as the placing of one or more wrapped foodstuffs in a second container, and the latter container itself. These definitions apply throughout this guide.*

Part 4
Note on legal references

Throughout this guide, the legal reference for the temperature control requirements is given as the Food Hygiene (England/Scotland/Wales/Northern Ireland) Regulations 2006, but it should be noted that this is actually four separate regulations, one for each country of the UK, i.e. Food Hygiene (England) Regulations 2006 (SI No. 2006/14), Food Hygiene (Scotland) Regulations 2006 (SSI No. 2006/3), Food Hygiene (Wales) Regulations 2006 (SI No. 2006/31), Food Hygiene (Northern Ireland) Regulations 2006 (SR No. 2006/3). These can be found at www.opsi.gov.uk. Throughout this guide, the key legal references are in bold and highlighted in boxes. An example is provided below.

> **Regulation (EC) No. 852/2004 on the Hygiene of Foodstuffs**
>
> **The temperature control requirements of the Food Hygiene (England/Scotland/ Wales/Northern Ireland) Regulations 2006**

Legal requirements

There are legal requirements in both EC Regulations and national legislation. The former set out the general requirements whilst national Regulations contain specific controls.

EC Regulations

Regulation (EC) No. 852/2004 on the Hygiene of Foodstuffs:

Article 4.2: Food business operators carrying out any stage of production, processing and distribution of food ... shall comply with the general hygiene requirements laid down in Annex II... .

Article 4.3: Food business operators shall, as appropriate, adopt the following specific hygiene measures ... compliance with temperature control requirements for foodstuffs ... maintenance of the cold chain.

Annex II Chapter IX.5: Raw materials, ingredients, intermediate products and finished products likely to support the reproduction of pathogenic micro-organisms or the formation of toxins are not to be kept at temperatures that might result in a risk to health. The cold chain is not to be interrupted. However, limited periods outside temperature control are permitted, to accommodate the practicalities of handling during preparation, transport, storage, display and service of food, provided that it does not result in a risk to health. Food businesses manufacturing, handling and wrapping processed foodstuffs are to have suitable rooms, large enough for the separate storage of raw materials from processed material and sufficient separate refrigerated storage.

National legislation

The temperature control requirements of the Food Hygiene (England/Scotland/Wales/Northern Ireland) Regulations 2006.

The temperature control requirements can be found in the Regulations as follows:

SI version	Regulation	Schedule
England	30	4
Wales	30	4
Northern Ireland	26	4
Scotland	30	4

These Regulations require certain foods to be held at temperatures that will prevent the growth of harmful bacteria or the formation of toxins. It is an offence to allow food to be kept at temperatures that would cause a risk to health, so you must make sure that any foods that need temperature control are kept at the right temperature.

The requirements of the English, Welsh and Northern Irish (E, W & NI) Regulations are the same but differ from the requirements in Scotland. One major difference is that in E, W & NI chilled foods are not to be kept above 8°C, but no temperature is defined for Scotland. Instead, food is to be kept "in a refrigerator or refrigerating chamber or in a cool ventilated place".

The E, W & NI Regulations contain an exemption from the 8°C or colder requirement for food "which, as part of a mail order transaction, is being conveyed to an ultimate consumer". However, they go on to specify that no person shall supply by mail order any food which is likely to support the growth of pathogenic micro-organisms or the formation of toxins and is being or has been conveyed by post or by a private or common carrier to an ultimate consumer, at a temperature which has given rise to, or is likely to give rise to, a risk to health.

A brief overview of the rest of the temperature control legislation is given in Appendix D, along with a list of the types of food covered by the Regulations.

Guide to compliance

Within a mail order operation, the temperature control requirements of the Food Hygiene (England/ Scotland/ Wales/Northern Ireland) Regulations 2006 apply, although the 8°C chilled holding requirement (E, W & NI) only applies up to the point of dispatch.

Prior to dispatch

Whilst limited periods outside temperature control are permitted to accommodate the practicalities of handling during preparation, storage or transport (prior to dispatch to the consumer), the acceptable limits will depend on the combination of time and temperature. Under normal circumstances, a single period of up to two hours is unlikely to be questioned.

In Scotland, as the regulations do not prescribe a chill holding temperature, the temperature deemed suitable will depend on a number of factors including: the type of food, how it has been prepared, what further preparation will take place and how long it will be held. Any instructions provided by the manufacturer will be relevant.

Conveyance to the ultimate consumer

During conveyance, there is no legal requirement to keep chilled food at 8°C or cooler. However, the food temperature must be maintained at a safe level. Thus, if it is likely to rise in transit above 8°C, the mail order operator should be confident that this is safe by reference to supporting technical or other data. Long established practices that have proved safe over many years are relevant in this context.

The exemption for food "which, as part of a mail order transaction, is being conveyed to an ultimate consumer" is only relevant in E, W & NI and only applies to supply to the ultimate consumer (public), not another food business operation or activity, such as a caterer. Thus for such deliveries, chilled food must be maintained at 8°C or cooler subject to the above two-hour exemption.

Points of clarification

All the temperature control provisions relate to the temperature of the **food** and not the air temperature of the holding unit. When decisions are to be made on the safety of a food, care should be taken to make sure that the readings taken represent the **food** temperature. This should be borne in mind before relying on temperature readouts fitted to refrigeration or other temperature-controlled equipment. Temperature measurements should be taken to check the relationship between the air temperature and the temperature of the food.

There may be some cases where the normal maximum temperature of 8°C will not be cold enough. Foods affected will ordinarily be marked with the lower temperature that must be observed, provided it is necessary for the safety of the food.

"Free samples" are not exempt from the temperature requirements.

Part 6 of this guide

The next section explains how to use HACCP principles to identify the hazards and controls for each food, on a case-by-case basis, taking into account all the relevant variables. These are likely to include the type of food, how it has been prepared, its specified shelf-life, type of packaging, temperature the packaged food can be expected to experience in transit and the time spent in transit.

Advice on good practice

At the time of dispatch, perishable foods should have as much of their shelf-life remaining as possible. Therefore, unless the product is frozen, the storage time prior to dispatch should be minimised and the holding temperature maintained within the range 0 to 5°C, i.e. significantly below the legal maximum of 8°C.

The mail order operator should agree with their supplier that the shelf-life applied to the food is appropriate for the temperatures the product will be subjected to throughout the operation, up to receipt by the consumer. During the warmer summer months, it may be prudent to apply a shorter shelf-life.

The packaging used in transit will clearly be a major factor in maintaining the food at a safe temperature. Appendix E (Packaging and conveyance to the consumer) contains advice on the kind of packaging and refrigerants available to businesses and how best to use them.

HACCP (hazard analysis and critical control points) is an internationally recognised approach to the successful management of food safety. However, the new requirement to implement procedures based on the principles of HACCP differs from the previous legal approach to food safety management before 2006, by introducing the need for the food safety management procedures to be documented, including record keeping, and the need for verification, whilst recognising the need for flexibility and proportionality.

In the context of this guide, the following approach would achieve compliance with the specific HACCP requirements of the regulations.

Legal requirements/ Guide to compliance

> **Regulation (EC) No. 852/2004 on the Hygiene of Foodstuffs**
>
> **Article 5 – Hazard analysis and critical control points**
>
> **Paragraph 1**
>
> **Food business operators shall put in place, implement and maintain a permanent procedure or procedures based on the HACCP principles.**

A mail order operator must establish, use and maintain, on a consistent and constant basis, food safety management procedures based on the principles of HACCP.

> **2. The HACCP principles referred to in paragraph 1 consist of the following:**
>
> **(a) identifying any hazards that must be prevented, eliminated or reduced to acceptable levels;**

A food hazard is anything that could cause harm to the consumer. There are three main categories of hazards that may arise in a mail order food operation. These are contamination of food by:

- bacteria or other micro-organisms that cause food poisoning, collectively known as pathogens
- chemicals, such as cleaning materials or pest baits
- foreign material, such as wood, plastic, metal, stone, glass, mouse droppings.

Of these, the most important hazard is likely to be pathogens that may contaminate and grow in food.

Hazards can vary between different mail order businesses depending on the source and range of foods sold, the wrapping and packaging of the food and the format and procedure for distributing the mail order product. Every mail order operator must identify the possible hazards for their own business, including foods brought in for resale.

> **(b) identifying the critical control points at the step or steps at which control is essential to prevent or eliminate a hazard or to reduce it to acceptable levels;**

It is helpful to divide the legal requirement into three stages:

- identifying steps (a "step" being a distinct, identifiable, separate stage, point, activity or process in the operation)
- identifying critical control points
- identifying and implementing controls.

A critical control point (CCP) is a step in the operation at which a control can be applied and at which this control is essential to prevent or eliminate a food safety hazard or to reduce it to an acceptable level. Sometimes to "prevent" is actually to "maintain" the status (safety) of the food. For example, when received into the mail order business a food should not contain more than a safe level of bacteria. This (safe) level must be maintained, i.e. the food is kept at a temperature to prevent the bacteria growing.

The primary focus must be on controlling and/or preventing the hazard manifesting itself in the food because within the context of this guide, the operating methods of mail order businesses are unlikely to be able to reduce or eliminate the contamination of a food once it has occurred.

Before any CCPs can be established, it is necessary to identify the individual steps in the operating process. In a mail order business these are likely to be, though not necessarily limited to, delivery and intake, storage, packaging process, pre-dispatch storage and delivery to the consumer.

Hazards can occur at any or all of the steps. For each type of food that the business handles, the hazards that may occur at each step should be identified. Controls must then be identified and implemented at each CCP.

Examples of the most likely hazards to occur and their respective controls are shown below.

Hazard

Food can become contaminated with micro-organisms, chemicals or foreign material.

Control

Controls will include clean equipment and storage areas, good personal hygiene of staff, and procedures to ensure food is protected from contamination by micro-organisms, foreign bodies or chemicals during handling and storage.

Hazard

Bacteria can grow if the food is held too long at the wrong temperatures.

Control

The time and temperature at which food is held, stored or displayed are all likely to be critical.

(c) establishing critical limits at critical control points which separate acceptability from unacceptability for the prevention, elimination or reduction of identified hazards;

A critical limit is defined as a criterion that separates acceptability from unacceptability. Where there are recognised technical or legal (e.g. temperature) numeric values that are applicable, the setting of critical limits can be relatively simple. As examples:

- technically it may be necessary to have a salt level of 3.5% (aqueous) throughout a vacuum packed food to control *Clostridium botulinum*
- the law may require that a particular food is stored at 8°C or colder.

However, for other controls it may not be possible to state a numeric value and a subjective, descriptive limit for acceptability will be necessary. As examples:

- "Staff are aware of and adhere to procedure"
- "Product to be used within shelf-life parameters".

(d) establishing and implementing effective monitoring procedures at critical control points;

When controls have been set, the critical control points should be monitored as frequently as necessary whenever that step is used. The types of hazards encountered can be controlled and monitored by taking basic measures. It is not necessary to measure the critical points against the critical limits every time a step is performed. It may be enough to do checks at appropriate intervals.

Checking temperatures of chilled product and equipment at the time of delivery, during storage and prior to dispatch are the most important monitoring procedures in relation to chilled pre-packaged mail order foods. Checking temperatures does not always involve probing with a thermometer. Delivery vehicles or chilled storage may be fitted with temperature readouts, and these can be checked.

(**Note:** Air temperature measurements do not always reflect the temperature of food at every part of the store, storage unit or vehicle. Occasional cross-checks – air versus food temperatures – should be made.)

Some controls will be the same for many different foods and this makes monitoring very much easier. It does not have to be done item by item. For example, when a number of perishable foods are kept under refrigeration, at 8°C or cooler, one storage temperature measurement should normally cover all the various foods in that fridge.

A CCP for mail order businesses is at the transportation/delivery to the consumer step in the operation. It would be prudent for the proprietor of a mail order business to have positive evidence to demonstrate that the safety of the food they purvey is not compromised by this aspect of the supply chain. It is already clear that controls for this essential stage are required but monitoring is equally important. One approach is to undertake test deliveries (see Advice on good practice on page 25).

Other critical controls can be more difficult to measure – e.g. cleaning and sanitation of equipment or the personal hygiene of staff. However, these can be vital to the safety of food, so there should be regular checks to ensure that standards are maintained. This may simply be by visual observations.

> **(e) establishing corrective actions when monitoring indicates that a critical control point is not under control;**

It is important to take corrective action if the critical limits are being exceeded or the controls are clearly not working. For example:

- out of specification deliveries to the business – review results/reject the food, as appropriate

- inadequate/poor cleaning – remove from service and re-clean

- out of specification refrigeration temperature – remove product to a working unit and adjust or repair the faulty equipment. (**Note**: high-risk products may need to be discarded if out of refrigeration for too long)

- infestation – in-depth housekeeping and adequate pest control.

Corrective action should be taken as soon as controls are found not to conform to the critical limits, i.e. "immediate operator corrective action". However, there may be corrective action that only management has the internal authority to make – for instance, if there are consistent failings in controls and they and/or the critical limits need to be reviewed and amended, i.e. "future management corrective action". (See the HACCP chart starting on page 16.)

> **(f) establishing procedures, which shall be carried out regularly, to verify that the measures outlined in subparagraphs (a) to (e) are working effectively;**

Verification is defined as: checking, by examination and the consideration of objective evidence, whether specified requirements have been fulfilled.

Verification is most likely to be undertaken by the management of the business and consist of reviews and observations to check the correct application and effectiveness of the food safety management procedures. The frequency of these verification procedures will vary from business to business and between different elements of the HACCP procedures. For example:

- as the performance of delivery into the mail order operation may not be under the direct influence of the management of that business, it may be appropriate to review each week the results of controls on deliveries (e.g. temperature of incoming product)

- if the packaging process is relatively simple and supervised by the owner of the mail order business, it may be appropriate for the packaging process records and procedures to be reviewed only twice per year

- again, a step within the operation that is largely outside the direct control of the mail order business is "delivery to consumer". Therefore, it would be sensible to review the carrier's performance at least twice a year

- if temperature checks are a key part of the food safety management procedures, then it is important to verify the accuracy of any thermometer relied on in such checks. (See Appendix F, Taking temperatures.)

> **(g) establishing documents and records commensurate with the nature and size of the food business to demonstrate the effective application of the measures outlined in subparagraphs (a) to (f).**

Key elements of documents and records, from a business perspective, are that:

i)   the management can demonstrate that the business is operating responsibly and legally

ii) the documentation process is not burdensome and is commensurate with the nature and size of the business

iii) the records can be used to enhance and develop the business.

In the past, businesses have voluntarily documented their hazard analysis and recorded the findings of their monitoring. Now both are a mandatory requirement.

The documenting of a food safety management procedure based on the principles of HACCP does not have to be substantial or complicated; indeed the opposites are desirable. It is essential that any records that are kept are accurate and truly reflect what is happening in the business.

Documentation needed to comply with the legal requirement

The procedure: if the business operator is following this guide, a HACCP chart similar to that given below will suffice.

Records of monitoring, corrective actions, verification and reviews

The traditional approach to record keeping has been to record all the measurements that have been taken. However, it is also important to record what is done when a non-conformance is encountered.

Thus, with paragraphs (ii) and (iii) above in mind, an alternative approach is to record only non-conformances and what corrective action was undertaken. The business management will need to be confident that they can achieve paragraph (i) whilst using this approach. They may want to have a person sign each day that the operation had been operating to the food safety management plan – i.e. that it was under control. Any of these records could simply be recorded in a "day book"/diary or another existing log of events.

> **When any modification is made in the product, process, or any step, food business operators shall review the procedure and make the necessary changes to it.**

It is not satisfactory to go through this process once and then forget about it. This part of the Regulation says that it must be kept up to date. From time to time the system should be reviewed and, if necessary, amended. For example:

- to check if the procedures put in place are actually working, or if unauthorised working practices have crept in over time
- the procedures must be reviewed if there is a material/significant change, for example:
  - the type of packaging used is changed
  - the carrier is changed
  - the product mix within a standard collection changes – e.g. in a hamper the balance of ambient foods to chilled foods shifts
  - a different food is sourced and sold by mail order.

> **4. Food business operators shall:**
>
> **(a) provide the competent authority with evidence of their compliance with paragraph 1 in the manner that the competent authority requires, taking account of the nature and size of the food business;**

Mail order business operators are required to provide their local authority enforcement officer with evidence that they have put in place, implemented and maintained a permanent procedure or procedures based on the HACCP principles, taking account of the nature and size of the food business. Documents provide evidence of the procedures put in place, while records demonstrate (verify) monitoring of those procedures and any corrective actions made in practice.

Guide to compliance

Documentation and record-keeping requirements are flexible and should relate to the size and nature of the business. For this reason the precise nature of documents and records is not prescribed in the law. A simple system limited to what is essential for food safety can be effective.

Advice on good practice

The *Practice Guidance for Enforcement Officers*, issued by the Food Standards Agency, provides advice on what enforcement officers could expect to find.

To meet the suggested expectations, mail order operators, as good practice, should be able:

a) to provide evidence that the person responsible for food safety has thought about their business and identified significant hazards and knows how to control them

b) to provide evidence that the business is following procedures that include steps where the significant hazards are controlled – for many businesses it may be appropriate to follow standard advice

c) to provide evidence that the business is monitoring their procedures, using physical checks (e.g. noting temperatures) and/or via visual checks (e.g. noting that the correct procedure is used). The person responsible for food safety should be able to explain the chosen method of monitoring

d) when the person responsible for food safety management is questioned, to explain how they ensure there is adequate supervision of staff and equipment, so as to assure that procedures are being followed and safe food dispatched, plus that when things go wrong appropriate action is taken

e) to provide evidence that the procedures in a business are reviewed to ensure they continue to represent good practice and reflect changes in the business

f) to provide documentation that is up to date and describes the main procedures or methods used in the business to control the most significant hazards

g) to provide periodic records that represent evidence that the procedures were followed. **Note:** Such records do not have to record every monitoring and supervisory activity.

The *Practice Guidance* makes it very clear that it is acceptable for a business to follow standard guidance issued for an industry sector, e.g. a guide such as this one, in order to meet the aforementioned expectations.

> **b)   ensure that any documents describing the procedures developed in accordance with this Article are up to date at all times;**

The food safety management procedure – e.g. a HACCP chart similar to that given below – should be applicable to the product being dispatched on any one day.

> **c)   retain any other documents and records for an appropriate period.**

This guide considers 13 months to be appropriate but a shorter period may be agreed with your local enforcement officer.

Food safety management chart based on the principles of HACCP

The following food safety management analysis assumes the food product is already within its primary wrapper.

As with the rest of the guide, the primary purpose is to address the safety of foods to which a *"use by"* date would have to be applied, if the prepacked food was sold at retail.

The HACCP chart in Table 2 both summarises and expands on the guide to compliance set out above. Overall, it is in itself a guide to compliance but the frequencies given for checks and verification procedures are advice on good practice.

Some elements may not be applicable to all businesses. For example, it may be appropriate for a business that manufactures/processes the product it sells by mail order to commence the food safety management process for the mail order part of its operation at step 2 or 3.

Further guidance and explanation of its content is given after the chart. This is an integral part of the chart.

It should be noted here that for non-destructive (between-pack) temperature readings, *Practice*

Guide to compliance

The following is further guidance and explanation of the HACCP chart's content and is an integral part of it.

Standard of facilities used

- Appendix C gives a summary of the general legal requirements.

- Perishable foods that remain liable to contamination (i.e. that are not vacuum-packed or in some other way hermetically sealed) should be prepared for final dispatch in similar facilities and by staff operating to the same standards of personal hygiene as would apply to manufacture/ processing of the food.

- Hermetically sealed foods should be packed in an area that is sound, well maintained and free from infestation. The area must be kept clean and tidy, in line with good hygiene practice, and have adequate handwashing and toilet facilities readily available.

- The establishment will need to be registered with the environmental health service of the local authority.

Infected food handlers

- Having been notified that a food handler has an infection – see the Staff section in Appendix C – management must then decide whether there is "safe work" that the staff member can undertake, i.e. work that does not involve direct contact with open food or with surfaces and equipment in areas where open food is stored or processed. "Safe work" would apply to all the elements of operations covered by this guide except the preparation and handling of gel refrigerants and the packing of non-hermetically sealed foods.

Transportation to the consumer

- The requirements for conveyances and/or containers used for transporting food are summarised in Appendix C. However, as explained in Appendix E, carriers will rarely convey mail order chilled foods in a vehicle specially designated to transport food.

- This situation is not counter to the hygiene legislation because the principle is that foodstuffs must be protected from contamination and maintained at appropriate temperatures. In the case of foods sold by mail order, such protection must be inherent in the regime used for the packaging of the food.

Infestation

- Can be caused by rodents, insects or birds.

Advice on good practice

Shelf-life

- A fundamental element of both ensuring food safety and commercial prudence is the need for the product, at intake, to have sufficient shelf-life remaining to allow for the time required for storage, packing, dispatch and transit to the consumer, whilst giving the consumer sufficient time to use it before its *use by* date.

- Given the wide range of perishable foods sold by mail order, plus the variations in style and size of mail order operations, it is not possible to give precise guidance here. However, it is essential that shelf-life be established on technically sound principles. Suitable data should be available to justify the shelf-life/*use by* date allotted. See also Advice on good practice in respect of temperature controls in Part 5.

- One such principle is that for vacuum or modified atmosphere-packaged foods, where chill temperatures (warmer than 3°C but cooler than 8°C) alone are used to control *Clostridium botulinum*, a maximum total shelf-life of 10 days should be assigned.

- In mixed packages of perishable foods, the delivery to the consumer regime should be based on the shortest shelf-life.

- In extreme conditions of hot weather, it may be prudent to substitute ambient stable products, if this is a viable alternative.

High-risk products

- For specific high-risk products, e.g. vacuum-packed foods, special precautions may be required to ensure a satisfactory product. Advice should be sought from your supplier, your local environmental health service, enforcement officer or other expert. For vacuum- or modified atmosphere-packaged foods, the Industry Code, namely the Campden and Chorleywood Food Research Association, Guideline No. 11: A Code of Practice for the Manufacture of Vacuum and Modified Atmosphere Packaged Chilled Foods (May 1996), can be consulted. Available from CCFRA on 01386 842048.

- Whatever aspect of the product you are relying on to ensure the product is safe to eat when it arrives with the consumer (e.g. temperature and/or salt content and/or acidity and/or water activity), check that this aspect is accurately in place at least twice per year.

- Live shellfish have their own particular purification and packaging requirements and should therefore be treated as a special case. Expert advice should be sought, especially for products that may be consumed raw (e.g. oysters).

Delivery to the consumer

- More advice on good practice is given in Appendix E.

- It should be noted that as there is a separate legal obligation on the seller, under the Sale of Goods Act, to refund or replace any product that is sub-standard on arrival at the consumer, there is the maximum commercial incentive to ensure strict adherence to the food safety management system.

Test deliveries

- Use a perishable food typical of the product range, sent under the standard regime agreed with the carrier, to a pre-arranged "dummy consumer", who is in a position to check whatever parameter is deemed important. The dummy consumer could be a relation or an employee. However, to achieve a more independent view a business colleague, a fellow trade association member, your packaging supplier or an independent laboratory might be chosen.

- If the temperature at which the food is received is important, then the "consumer" will need to have an accurate method for measuring this. If a temperature logger is used (see Appendix F) the recipient may only need to return the equipment. The frequency of such monitoring will depend on a range of factors, e.g. throughput of the business, complaint levels, weather conditions. At least one test should be carried out during the summer. Proof of the effectiveness of the packaging/delivery regime under the worst-case conditions would be the ideal.

Taking temperatures

- See Appendix F.

Part 7

Training

A food business operator/proprietor must address the supervision and instruction and/or training of both **food hygiene** and **food safety management**.

Food safety is the responsibility of everyone involved in the storage, packing and dispatch of mail order foods, and all those staff must have an appropriate understanding of good food hygiene and food safety hazards, relevant to the food they work with, and how they are controlled.

It is important to recognise that supervisors and managers can undermine any amount of supervision, instruction or training if not suitably trained themselves.

Legal requirements

> **Regulation (EC) No. 852/2004 on the Hygiene of Foodstuffs, Chapter XII of Annex II**
>
> **TRAINING**
>
> **Food business operators are to ensure:**
>
> 1. **That food handlers are supervised and instructed and/or trained in food hygiene matters commensurate with their work activity;**
>
> 2. **That those responsible for the development and maintenance of the procedure referred to in Article 5(1) of this Regulation or for the operation of relevant guides have received adequate training in the application of the HACCP principles**

This guide provides a model system for implementing the legal requirements, but not all of what is said will apply equally to all businesses. The overall approach is recommended as a guide, and it would be possible for a food business to demonstrate to enforcers that it had satisfied the legal requirements in other ways.

The legal requirement, in respect of food hygiene, has been in force since September 1995.

Guide to compliance

Supervision and instruction and/or training of food handlers

The requirement in Annex II, Chapter XII, paragraph 1 of Regulation 852/2004 applies only to food handlers. For the purposes of this guide a food handler is anyone who handles wrapped or packaged food, packaging and other food equipment, including surfaces. The handling or preparation of open foods is outside the scope of this guide.

Food business operators must ensure that food handlers receive instruction and/or training in food hygiene appropriate to their food-handling duties. The training and/or instruction provided should ensure that food handlers have sufficient knowledge and competence to handle food safely. In addition, all food handlers must be supervised to an appropriate level (see further guidance below).

There is no legal requirement for staff to attend formal training courses or obtain a qualification. The appropriate knowledge and competencies can be obtained in a number of ways, including on-the-job training, self-study through expertly produced guidance materials, attendance on formal training courses or prior experience.

Where necessary, appropriate arrangements should be made for staff whose first language is not English and/or staff with learning or literacy difficulties.

The following guidance explains what food handlers need to know, and by when, in order to comply with the legal requirements.

Whom	Staff who handle wrapped food at intake, in storage or during packing, including those with a supervisory role	
What	Instruction in the essentials of food hygiene	Instruction and/or training pertinent to job
When	Before starting work for the first time	Within four weeks of starting work

Content: the essentials of food hygiene

- Keep yourself clean and wear clean clothing.
- Always wash your hands thoroughly before handling food, after using the toilet, handling raw foods or waste, before starting work, after every break.
- Tell your supervisor, before commencing work, of any skin, nose, throat, stomach or bowel trouble or infected wound.
- Ensure cuts and sores are covered with a waterproof, high-visibility dressing.
- Do not smoke or spit where food, its packaging or refrigerant is stored or handled.
- Follow any food safety instructions from your supervisor.
- Keep perishable food refrigerated.
- Keep your workplace clean and tidy.
- Report any sightings of pest activity.
- If you see something wrong, tell your supervisor.

These points can be amended to suit each business. Some points may not be relevant to some mail order businesses.

Content: instruction or training pertinent to job

- Cold chain maintenance.
- Stock control regimes.
- Good hygiene practice.
- The food safety standards and procedures that the business applies to deliveries and intake, storage, packaging process, pre-dispatch storage and dispatch.

Supervision

All staff should be properly supervised and instructed to ensure that they work hygienically and in accordance with the business's food safety procedures.

The level of supervision should depend on the competence and experience of the individual food handler. Where an operation employs only one or two people, supervision may not be practical. In such cases, training and/or instruction should be sufficient to allow work to be unsupervised.

Training in the application of HACCP principles

The food business operator must ensure that those within the business responsible for developing and maintaining the HACCP-based food safety management procedures or for the operation of relevant guides are appropriately trained.

As in the case of food handler training or instruction, food business operators are responsible for determining how training in HACCP principles or the operation of relevant guides is achieved. There is no legal requirement for staff to attend formal training courses or obtain a qualification. The appropriate knowledge and competencies can be obtained in a number of ways, including on-the-job training, self-study through expertly produced guidance materials, attendance on formal training courses or prior experience.

The following two options would represent compliance with the regulations:

Option 1

Whom	A person(s), most likely to be a manager or supervisor, who develops and maintains the food safety procedures
What	Training in the application of the HACCP principles
When	In advance of taking on the responsibility

Training content

The training content should relate to the specific food operations in the business. It should be sufficient to ensure the staff concerned can develop and maintain the business's HACCP food safety management procedures. It is considered that such training would need to cover:

- identification of relevant food hazards in the business
- selection of valid control measures and their application

- monitoring the controls to ensure they are working effectively, and what to do if they are not
- documenting the HACCP procedures and deciding what records to keep to show the procedures are working
- reviewing the HACCP procedures to ensure they remain up to date.

Option 2

Whom	A person(s), most likely to be a manager or supervisor, who operates food safety procedures based on a relevant guide – e.g. this guide
What	Instruction and/or training in the content and application of a relevant guide
When	In advance of taking on the responsibility

Training content

This *Industry Guide to Good Hygiene Practice* for mail order foods constitutes a relevant guide. If a business is operating HACCP procedures based on the advice in this guide, the training content should aim to familiarise relevant staff with the content and application of Part 6 of this guide: Application of food safety management procedures based on the principles of HACCP.

New employees/seasonal/agency staff

Employees must be instructed on how to do their specific job hygienically. If they claim to have been trained previously, they should be able to provide evidence of this. In cases where such evidence is not available, it should be assumed that the employee is untrained and they should receive the appropriate instruction and/or training within the timescales shown above. Instruction in the basic awareness of hygiene principles (the essentials of food hygiene) must be given at induction before staff engage in any food-handling activities. Pending any further training that is deemed necessary, staff must be adequately supervised to ensure safe handling practices are maintained. This guidance is also relevant to new, seasonal or agency staff responsible for developing, maintaining or operating the HACCP-based food safety management procedures.

Advice on good practice

Whom	Supervisors who do not handle food
What	Instruction and/or training pertinent to job
When	Within four weeks of starting the supervisory role

Content: instruction and/or training pertinent to job

- Time/temperature and food spoilage principles.
- Cold chain maintenance.
- Role of packaging and refrigerant.
- Taking of temperatures.
- Stock control regimes.
- The applicable standards the business applies to deliveries and intake, storage, packaging process, pre-dispatch storage and dispatch.
- Specific CCP responsibilities.
- Good hygiene practices.
- Pest control awareness.

General principles

As a matter of good practice, instruction and/or training in hygiene and the operation of HACCP principles should be consistent with any relevant National Occupational Standards.

It is good practice that all training should be given by qualified and competent persons who have been trained to train food handlers.

Training plan and records

It is good practice for a business to have a plan to identify the training needed for each member of staff. In addition, it is good practice to keep records of the training completed by each member of staff. These records are likely to form part of the evidence the business would use to demonstrate it has a satisfactory food safety management system, based on the principles of HACCP. Also, evidence of training in hygiene and food safety management may be very important in demonstrating compliance with the legal requirements.

Records may also be relevant when attempting to establish a "due diligence" defence.

Training needs should be reviewed on a regular basis. Update training may be necessary at intervals.

When considering in-house training, businesses will find it beneficial to have documented course instruction notes. This will help to ensure consistency in training over time and will demonstrate a disciplined approach to the subject.

Other staff

Other staff who are not food handlers may also need instruction, supervision or training as a matter of good practice. This may include cleaners, engineers, maintenance fitters and any other support staff who visit the operation.

They should understand the basic hygiene principles (the essentials of food hygiene), as part of their induction to the job.

Part 8
Appendices

Appendix A
The application of a *use by* date

The Food Standards Agency has issued guidance on when to give a *use by* date on food labels of prepacked foods. The following is based on this guidance but the full document is available at www.food.gov.uk.

The Food Labelling Directive (2000/13/EEC) requires that a *use by* rather than a *best before* date should be used on those prepacked foods "which, from the microbiological point of view, are highly perishable and are therefore likely after a short period to constitute an immediate danger to human health". It is important to note that both criteria – time and danger – have to be satisfied.

Foods that need labelling with *use by* dates are those that have to be stored at low temperatures **to maintain their safety rather than their quality.** They will have a short product life following manufacture, after which their consumption may present a risk of food poisoning. They will be likely to fall into one or both of the following groups:

- foods that, at ambient or chill temperatures, are capable of supporting the formation of toxins or multiplication of pathogens to a level that could lead to food poisoning if they are not stored correctly

- foods intended for consumption either without cooking or after treatment (such as reheating) unlikely to be sufficient to destroy food-poisoning organisms that may be present.

The table on the next page indicates which foods will generally need a *use by* date.

Other foods that are likely to require a *use by* date are uncooked products comprising or containing either meat, poultry or fish, and foods packed in a vacuum or modified atmosphere and held at chill temperatures to keep them safe. Prepacked fresh poultry meat is required to bear a *use by* date under the terms of EC Regulations. Under the latter, eggs require marking with a *best before* rather than a *use by* date (the date up to and including which the foodstuff will retain its optimum condition, e.g. it will not be stale).

Foods that generally need a *use by* date

Food category	Examples
Dairy products	• Soft or semi-hard cheese ripened by moulds and/or bacteria once the ripening or maturation is completed. • Dairy-based desserts (including milk substitutes), such as fromage frais, mousses, crème caramels, products containing whipped cream. • Unless the pH of the product would prevent the growth of pathogenic micro-organisms or the formation of toxins, or unless other effective preservative mechanisms are present.
Cooked products	• Products, including sandwiches, containing or comprising cooked meat, poultry, fish, eggs (or substitutes for meat, poultry, fish or eggs), milk, hard and soft cheese, cereals (including rice), pulses and vegetables, whether or not they are intended to be eaten without further reheating.
Smoked or cured fish	
Smoked or cured ready-to-eat meat that is not shelf-stable at room temperature	• Sliced, cured, cooked meats such as hams, some salamis and other fermented sausages, depending on the method of curing.
Prepared ready-to-eat foods	• Prepared vegetables, vegetable salads containing fruit, or prepared salads (such as coleslaw) containing other products and prepared products such as mayonnaise.
Uncooked or partly cooked pastry and dough products	• Pizzas, sausage rolls or fresh pasta containing meat, poultry, fish (or substitutes for meat, poultry or fish) or vegetables.

Appendix B
General Food Regulations 2004 – product recall and notification requirement

These Regulations applied from 1st January 2005 and aid the implementation of the EU Regulation 178/2002.

Article 19 of the latter places obligations on food businesses to recall and/or withdraw food from the market if it is not in compliance with food safety requirements. The business must also notify the local enforcement authority and the Food Standards Agency as soon as possible. This applies to retailers in certain circumstances, e.g. where they are responsible for the manufacture or sole distribution of a product.

Where retailers sell a branded product that does not meet the food safety requirements, the brand owners will be responsible for notification and withdrawal/recall.

Where products may have reached the consumer, there is an obligation on food businesses to inform consumers of the reason for the withdrawal of the product and, where necessary, recall products already supplied. Mail order operators must be able to undertake a fast and accurate product recall when necessary. Hence, address details of both purchasers and gift recipients should be retained for a suitable period. In order to restrict the quantities involved, operators should consider the most appropriate batch size they would wish to identify.

A guidance document to accompany the Regulations is available from the Food Standards Agency at www.food.gov.uk/foodindustry/guidancenotes

Appendix C
Regulation (EC) No. 852/2004 on the Hygiene of Foodstuffs – a brief summary

This Regulation sets out basic hygiene requirements for all aspects of your business, from your premises and facilities to the personal hygiene of your staff. The following sections contain a brief summary of the main requirements of the Regulation. The applicability of any particular section may vary from business to business.

Food premises

Premises of food businesses should be kept clean, and in good repair and condition. The following table sets out more specific requirements for premises.

Subject	What you must do	Part of the Regulation
Layout, design, construction and size	Make sure the premises permit good hygiene practice and easy cleaning, and protect food against external sources of contamination, such as pests. Ensure that there are, where necessary, suitable temperature-controlled handling and storage conditions of sufficient capacity for maintaining foodstuffs at appropriate temperatures and designed to allow those temperatures to be monitored and, where necessary, recorded.	Annex II Chapter I.2
Toilets	There must be an adequate number of toilets and these must not lead directly into food areas.	Annex II Chapter I.3
Handwashing facilities and washbasins	Make sure there are an adequate number of washbasins available, designated for cleaning hands. Make sure that basins have hot and cold (or appropriately mixed) running water. You must provide materials for cleaning and hygienically drying hands. Where necessary, facilities for washing food must be separate from handwashing facilities.	Annex II Chapter I.4
Ventilation	Make sure there is suitable and sufficient ventilation, either natural or mechanical. Ventilation systems must be accessible for cleaning and/or replacement of parts.	Annex II Chapter I.5
Ventilation of toilets	All toilets inside food premises must have adequate ventilation, either natural or mechanical.	Annex II Chapter I.6
Lighting	Make sure the premises have adequate natural and/or artificial lighting.	Annex II Chapter I.7
Drainage	Make sure there are adequate drainage facilities. Where drainage channels are open, waste must not flow from a contaminated area towards or into a clean area.	Annex II Chapter I.8
Changing facilities	Where necessary, you must provide adequate changing facilities for staff.	Annex II Chapter I.9
Cleaning agents and disinfectants	Make sure these are not stored in areas where food is handled.	Annex II Chapter I.10

Food rooms

The design and layout of rooms where food is prepared, treated or processed – excluding food storage rooms, packaging areas for wrapped food and dining areas, but including rooms contained in means of transport – must permit good hygiene, including protection against contamination between and during operations.

Subject	What you must do	Part of the Regulation
Floors, walls and surfaces	Make sure floors, walls and surfaces in contact with food are maintained in a sound condition. They must be easy to clean and, where necessary, to disinfect.	Annex II Chapter II.1 (a) (b) and (f)
Ceilings	The design and construction of ceilings should prevent accumulation of dirt, condensation, growth of moulds and shedding of particles.	Annex II Chapter II.1 (c)
Windows	Windows must be constructed to prevent the accumulation of dirt. Where necessary, windows that can be opened to the outside must be fitted with insect-proof screens.	Annex II Chapter II.1 (d)
Doors	Doors must be easy to clean and, where necessary, to disinfect.	Annex II Chapter II.1 (e)
Cleaning, disinfecting and storage of tools, utensils and equipment	You must provide adequate facilities for cleaning, disinfecting and storing tools, utensils and equipment, where necessary. There must be an adequate supply of hot and cold water.	Annex II Chapter II.2
Washing food	Where appropriate, you must provide adequate facilities for washing food, including a supply of hot and/or cold potable (drinking) water as required.	Annex II Chapter II.3

Movable/temporary premises

There are different requirements for:

- movable and/or temporary premises – e.g. marquees, market stalls, mobile sales vehicles
- vending machines
- domestic premises used primarily as a "private dwelling house"
- premises used occasionally for catering purposes.

Subject	What you must do	Part of the Regulation
Premises and vending machines	Make sure that these are sited, designed, constructed, kept clean and maintained in good repair, so as to avoid the risk of contaminating food, especially by animals and pests.	Annex II Chapter III.1
Personal hygiene facilities	Provide appropriate facilities to maintain adequate personal hygiene, where necessary.	Annex II Chapter III.2 (a)
Surfaces	Make sure that surfaces in contact with food are easy to clean and, where necessary, to disinfect.	Annex II Chapter III.2 (b)
Cleaning of utensils and equipment	Make adequate provision for the cleaning and, where necessary, disinfecting of utensils and equipment.	Annex II Chapter III.2 (c)
Cleaning of foodstuffs	Make adequate provision for the cleaning of foodstuffs, where necessary.	Annex II Chapter III.2 (d)
Hot and cold running water	Make available an adequate supply of hot and/or cold potable (drinking) water, where necessary.	Annex II Chapter III.2 (e)
Waste storage and disposal	Make adequate arrangements for storage and disposal of waste, where necessary.	Annex II Chapter III.2 (f)
Temperature control	Have adequate facilities for maintaining and monitoring suitable temperature conditions.	Annex II Chapter III.2 (g)
Avoiding contamination	Place foods where the risk of contamination will be avoided, as far as is practical.	Annex II Chapter III.2 (h)

Transport

Food must always be transported in a way that minimises the risk of contamination.

Subject	What you must do	Part of the Regulation
Containers and vehicles used for transport of food	Any container or vehicle used for transporting foodstuffs must be kept clean and maintained in good repair to protect food from contamination. Where necessary, the container or vehicle must be designed and constructed to permit adequate cleaning and/or disinfection.	Annex II Chapter IV.1
Dedicated containers	Receptacles in vehicles and/or containers must not be used for transporting anything other than foodstuffs, where this may result in contamination of foodstuffs.	Annex II Chapter IV.2
Containers or vehicles used for different foodstuffs or for both food and non-food products at the same time	You must separate products effectively, where necessary, to protect against the risk of contamination.	Annex II Chapter IV.3
Bulk transport of food in liquid, granulated or powder form	Bulk foodstuffs in liquid, granulated or powder form must be transported in receptacles and/or containers/tankers reserved for the transport of foodstuffs, if otherwise there is a risk of contamination. Containers reserved for foodstuffs must be marked clearly to show they are used only for foodstuffs.	Annex II Chapter IV.4
Containers or vehicles used for non-food products or different foodstuffs	You must clean the containers/vehicles effectively between loads to avoid the risk of contamination.	Annex II Chapter IV.5
Minimises the risk of contamination	Foodstuffs in conveyances or containers must be placed and protected in a way that minimises the risk of contamination.	Annex II Chapter IV.6
Maintaining and monitoring temperatures	Where necessary, vehicles and/or containers used for transporting foodstuffs must be capable of keeping foodstuffs at appropriate temperatures. Where necessary, the vehicle and/or container must be designed to allow those temperatures to be monitored.	Annex II Chapter IV.7

Equipment

All articles, fittings and equipment that come into contact with food must be kept clean.

Subject	What you must do	Part of the Regulation
Cleaning of equipment	Equipment, articles and fittings must be effectively cleaned and, where necessary, disinfected. Cleaning and disinfection must take place at a frequency sufficient to avoid any risk of contamination.	Annex II Chapter V.1 (a)
Minimising contamination	Make sure that all articles, fittings and equipment that come into contact with food are constructed, made of such materials and kept in good repair, so as to minimise the risk of any contamination of the food.	Annex II Chapter V.1 (b)
Construction to allow cleaning and disinfection	All articles, fittings and equipment that come into contact with food must be constructed, made of such materials and kept in good repair, so as to enable them to be kept thoroughly cleaned and, where necessary, disinfected.	Annex II Chapter V.1 (c)
Installation	All articles, fittings and equipment that come into contact with food must be installed in a way that allows adequate cleaning of the surrounding area.	Annex II Chapter V.1 (d)
Control devices	Where necessary, equipment must be fitted with any appropriate control device to guarantee fulfilment of the objectives of this Hygiene of Foodstuffs Regulation.	Annex II Chapter V.2
Chemical additives	Where chemical additives have to be used to prevent corrosion of equipment and containers, they must be used in accordance with good practice.	Annex II Chapter V.3

Waste

The storage and disposal of waste can present a risk of contaminating food, so you must make sure you follow the requirements of the Regulation.

Subject	What you must do	Part of the Regulation
Food and other waste	Food waste, non-edible by-products and other refuse are to be removed from rooms where food is present as quickly as possible, so as to avoid their accumulation.	Annex II Chapter VI.1
Containers for waste	Make sure that containers can be closed, unless the environmental health services are satisfied that this is not appropriate. The containers must be capable of being cleaned and, where necessary, disinfected.	Annex II Chapter VI.2
Arrangements for the storage and removal of waste	You must make adequate provision for storage and disposal, in an hygienic and environmentally friendly way, of waste. The latter is not to constitute a direct or indirect source of contamination. Refuse stores must be designed and managed so as to enable them to be kept clean and, where necessary, free from animals and pests.	Annex II Chapter VI.3 and 4

Water supply

Subject	What you must do	Part of the Regulation
Water supply	There must be an adequate supply of potable (drinking) water. Use potable water in food preparation so that the food is not contaminated.	Annex II Chapter VII.1 (a)
Fishery products	Clean water* may be used with whole fishery products. Clean seawater** may be used with live bivalve molluscs, echinoderms, tunicates and marine gastropods. Clean water may also be used for external washing. When such water is used, adequate facilities are to be available for its supply. * "Clean water" means clean seawater and fresh water of a similar quality. ** "Clean seawater" means natural, artificial or purified seawater or brackish water that does not contain micro-organisms, harmful substances or toxic marine plankton in quantities capable of directly or indirectly affecting the health quality of food.	Annex II Chapter VII.1 (b)
Water unfit for drinking	Water unfit for drinking, e.g. for fire control, must be conducted separately from potable water.	Annex II Chapter VII.2
Recycled water	Recycled water used in processing or as an ingredient is not to present a risk of contamination. It is to be of the same standard as potable water, unless the environmental health services are satisfied that the quality of the water cannot affect the wholesomeness of the foodstuff in its finished form.	Annex II Chapter VII.3
Ice	Ice must be made from potable water or, when used to chill whole fishery products, clean water. It must be made, stored and handled appropriately to protect it from all contamination.	Annex II Chapter VII.4
Steam	Steam used directly in contact with food must not contain substances hazardous to health or likely to contaminate the product.	Annex II Chapter VII.5
Heat treatment of hermetically sealed containers	Where heat treatment is applied to foodstuffs in hermetically sealed containers, ensure that water used to cool the containers after heat treatment is not a source of contamination for the foodstuff.	Annex II Chapter VII.6

Staff

Subject	What you must do	Part of the Regulation
Personal hygiene	Everyone working in a food-handling area must maintain a high degree of personal cleanliness. They must wear suitable, clean and, where necessary, protective clothing.	Annex II Chapter VIII.1
Infected food handlers	Anyone suffering from, or being a carrier of, a disease likely to be transmitted through food or afflicted – for example, with infected wounds, skin infections, sores or diarrhoea – must not be permitted to handle food or enter any food-handling area in any capacity if there is any likelihood of direct or indirect contamination. Any person so affected and employed in a food business, and who is likely to come into contact with food, must immediately report the illness or symptoms, and if possible their causes, to the food business operator.	Annex II Chapter VIII.2

Provisions applicable to foodstuffs

Subject	What you must do	Part of the Regulation
Accepting raw materials	Do not accept any raw materials or ingredients, other than live animals, if you know or suspect that they are contaminated and would still be unfit after normal sorting or processing.	Annex II Chapter IX.1
Storing raw materials	Raw materials and ingredients must be stored in appropriate conditions designed to prevent harmful deterioration and protect them from contamination.	Annex II Chapter IX.2
Protecting against contamination	At all stages of production, processing and distribution, food must be protected against any contamination likely to render the food unfit for human consumption, injurious to health or contaminated in such a way that it would be unreasonable to expect it to be consumed in that state.	Annex II Chapter IX.3
Control of animals and pests	There must be adequate procedures to control pests and to prevent domestic animals from having access to places where food is prepared, handled or stored, unless the environmental health services permit special cases.	Annex II Chapter IX.4
Temperatures and segregation in storage	Raw materials, ingredients, intermediate products and finished products likely to support the reproduction of pathogenic micro-organisms or the formation of toxins must not be kept at temperatures that might result in a risk to health. The cold chain is not to be interrupted, except for limited periods to accommodate the practicalities of handling during preparation, transport, storage, display and service of food, provided that it does not result in a risk to health. Food businesses manufacturing, handling and wrapping processed foodstuffs are to have suitable rooms, large enough for the separate storage of raw materials from processed material and sufficient separate refrigerated storage.	Annex II Chapter IX.5
Cooling of food	Where food is to be held or served at chilled temperatures, it must be cooled as quickly as possible following the heat processing stage, or final preparation stage if no heat process is applied, to a temperature that does not result in a risk to health.	Annex II Chapter IX.6
Thawing of food	The thawing of food must be undertaken in such a way as to minimise the risk of growth of pathogenic micro-organisms or the formation of toxins in the foods. During thawing, foods are to be subjected to temperatures that would not result in a risk to health. Where run-off liquid from the thawing process may present a risk to health, it must be adequately drained. Following thawing, food is to be handled in such a manner as to minimise the risk of growth of pathogenic micro-organisms or the formation of toxins.	Annex II Chapter IX.7
Hazardous and/or inedible substances	Hazardous and/or inedible substances, including animal feedstuffs, must be adequately labelled and stored in separate and secure containers.	Annex II Chapter IX.8

Wrapping and packaging of foodstuffs

Subject	What you must do	Part of the Regulation
Packaging materials in general	Material used for wrapping and packaging must not be a source of contamination.	Annex II Chapter X.1
Storage of wrapping materials	Wrapping materials must be stored in such a manner that they are not exposed to a risk of contamination.	Annex II Chapter X.2
Wrapping and packaging operations	Wrapping and packaging operations must be carried out so as to avoid contamination of the products. Where appropriate, and in particular in the case of cans and glass jars, the integrity of the container's construction and its cleanliness must be assured.	Annex II Chapter X.3
Reusable material	Wrapping and packaging material reused for foodstuffs must be easy to clean and, where necessary, to disinfect.	Annex II Chapter X.4

Heat treatment

The following requirements apply only to food placed on the market in hermetically sealed containers.

Subject	What you must do	Part of the Regulation
Temperature achievement and contamination control	Any heat-treatment process used to process an unprocessed product, or to process further a processed product, must raise every part of the product treated to a given temperature for a given period of time and prevent the product from becoming contaminated during the process.	Annex II Chapter XI.1(a) and (b)
Monitoring	To ensure that the process employed achieves the desired objectives, food business operators must check regularly the main relevant parameters, particularly temperature, pressure, sealing and microbiology.	Annex II Chapter XI.2
Process specification	The process used should conform to an internationally recognised standard (e.g. pasteurisation, ultra high temperature or sterilisation).	Annex II Chapter XI.3

Training

Food business operators must ensure the following.

Subject	What you must do	Part of the Regulation
Supervision, instruction and training	All food handlers must be supervised and instructed and/or trained in food hygiene matters to a level appropriate to their job.	Annex II Chapter XII.1
Training in HACCP principles	Those responsible for the development and maintenance of the food safety management procedure based on the HACCP principles, required by this Regulation (Article 5), or the operation of relevant guides must have received adequate training in the application of the HACCP principles.	Annex II Chapter XII.2
Sector-specific training	Comply with any requirements of UK national law concerning training programmes for persons working in certain food sectors.	Annex II Chapter XII.3

Appendix D
Temperature control requirements of the Food Hygiene (England/Scotland/Wales/Northern Ireland) Regulations 2006 – a brief summary

These Regulations require certain foods to be held at temperatures that will prevent the growth of harmful bacteria or the formation of toxins. It is an offence to allow food to be kept at temperatures that would cause a risk to health, so you must make sure that any foods that need temperature control are kept at the right temperature.

Foods that need temperature control must be kept either hot at 63°C or hotter, or cold at 8°C or colder. Different rules apply in Scotland.

Foods that need temperature control

Generally foods that need temperature control will be marked with a *use by* date and will be labelled "keep refrigerated". Some of the products listed in Appendix A might be preserved or prepared in a way that changes the need for temperature control. The packaging will indicate this.

The table below shows the main categories of foods that need temperature control.

Dairy products	Dairy products must be kept chilled unless the packaging says they are "stable" at room temperature (in other words, they do not need to be chilled to stop them going off). Products requiring chilling include many types of milk, yoghurt, cream, foods with a cream filling, dairy-based desserts and certain cheeses.
Cooked products	Many cooked products must be kept chilled until ready to be eaten cold or heated. These include most foods containing eggs, meat, fish, dairy products, cereals, rice, pulses or vegetables. Sandwiches containing any of these ingredients also need to be chilled.
Smoked/cured ready-to-eat meat or fish	Most smoked or cured products must be kept chilled until ready to be eaten cold or heated. These include sliced cured meats like ham, unless the curing method means the product is not perishable at room temperature.
Prepared ready-to-eat foods	Prepared ready-to-eat foods must be kept chilled. These include prepared vegetables (chopped and washed), bags of salad leaves, vegetable salads such as coleslaw, and products containing mayonnaise.
Uncooked or partly cooked pastry and dough products	These include pizzas and fresh pasta containing meat, fish or vegetables. Products must be kept chilled until they are heated.

Foods that *do not* need to be chilled

These are the main categories of foods that are exempt from the national temperature control requirements. Other regulations that apply to products covered by Regulation 853/2004, laying down hygiene rules for products of animal origin, may require some of these categories of food to be chilled, e.g. raw meat.

Foods that can be kept at room temperature throughout their shelf-life, without causing any health risk	These include some cured/smoked products and certain bakery products. Some of these products can have a long shelf-life – e.g. naan breads and some desserts.
Food that goes through a preservation process	This includes most canned/dried foods, jams, pickles and sauces, which are not perishable at room temperature until the container is opened or the food, if necessary, is rehydrated.
Food that must be ripened or matured at room temperature	This includes soft or mould-ripened cheeses. But once they are fully ripened or matured, these foods must be chilled while they are stored and/or displayed.
Raw food intended for further processing (including cooking) that will ensure the food is fit for human consumption	This includes fresh meat, fish and shellfish, except where it is intended to be eaten raw – e.g. sushi. (However, some of these products need to be chilled if their quality, as opposed to their safety, is to be maintained.)
Mail order food	Food delivered by mail order does not need to be chilled during transit to the ultimate consumer. However, it must not be transported at temperatures that could cause a health risk.

Circumstances where food may be kept outside required temperatures

There are certain circumstances (listed below) where it may not be practical to keep foods at the required temperatures. So the Regulations allow you to keep food out of temperature control for limited periods of time.

Service or display	Food displayed in restaurants or cafes, put out on buffets, or served or displayed in shops can be kept out of temperature control for a limited time. However, you must take care not to exceed the maximum display times, because otherwise you could cause a risk to health.
	Foods that normally need to be kept chilled **can be kept unchilled for up to four hours**, to allow them to be served or displayed. Foods can only be kept unchilled for **one period of service or display**. After this, any food that is left must be thrown away or chilled until final use.
	Service and display would not generally be relevant to mail order foods.
During transfers, processing, preparation or packaging	Food can be kept unchilled for a limited time, consistent with food safety, when: • it is being transferred to or from premises and is in a vehicle used for the purposes of a food business • it is kept at a temperature above 8°C for an unavoidable reason – e.g. the defrosting of equipment, temporary breakdown of equipment or to accommodate the practicalities of handling during and after processing, preparation or packaging.
Regulations in Scotland	In Scotland, the Regulations apply slightly differently. A maximum temperature for chilling foods is not specified but businesses are still required to chill foods if they need to be chilled to keep them safe. Maximum times for keeping foods out of temperature control for service or display are not specified, for either hot or cold.
	Food can be kept unchilled for a limited time when: • it is being loaded or unloaded from a refrigerated vehicle to be delivered to/from food premises • there are unavoidable circumstances – e.g. when food has to be handled during and after processing, or if equipment is defrosted or temporarily breaks down.

Appendix E
Packaging and conveyance to the consumer

Legal requirements/ Guide to compliance

Regulation (EC) No. 852/2004 on the Hygiene of Foodstuffs:

Annex II Chapter X: Provisions applicable to the wrapping and packaging of foodstuffs

1. **Materials used for wrapping and packaging are not to be a source of contamination.**

2. **Wrapping materials are to be stored in such a manner that they are not exposed to a risk of contamination.**

3. **Wrapping and packaging operations are to be carried out so as to avoid contamination of the products. Where appropriate and in particular in the case of cans and glass jars, the integrity of the container's construction and its cleanliness is to be assured.**

4. **Wrapping and packaging material re-used for foodstuffs is to be easy to clean and, where necessary, to disinfect.**

This is a new legal requirement but has been inherent in the previous and ongoing need to avoid contamination of food.

By following the controls set out in the HACCP chart in Part 6 of this guide (see page 16), an operation would comply with Annex II Chapter X.

Advice on good practice

There is a distinct relationship between the all-important, achievement of customer/consumer satisfaction and the packaging system chosen, its labelling, the carrier performance, product shelf-life and the general provision of information to the recipient. Of course, the customer and the actual consumer may often not be one and the same.

Destination details

An accurate name and address is essential in order to minimise the risk of delayed delivery. Systems should be in place to help ensure the name and address are accurate – e.g. a specific "box" for the post code, always reading back and spelling out the details provided in a telephone order, and asking for telephone contact details for both customer and consumer. Checking the delivery address against one or more address databases could help eliminate unforeseen inaccuracies. If the system is computer-based, checking can be very quick.

Packaging system once product is wrapped

It would be unusual if there were not a trade-off between cost and performance and, for certain mail order businesses, visual impact for the particular style. However, as can be seen in the food safety management procedure section of this guide, there are goals that need to be achieved in order to safeguard product safety.

The primary requirement is for a well-insulated outer packaging, which is sufficiently robust to prevent it, the contents or the temperature seal from being damaged and thus avoid contamination of the food or loss of temperature control. Where a more sophisticated package is appropriate or demanded, combined packaging and refrigerant systems are available. For these, some manufacturers offer to supply a validated certificate of temperature control, using their in-house calibration facilities or by the provision of a computer programme to be used by their customers.

Refrigerant

The key requirement is for the food to be safe to eat within the allotted shelf-life. The need for refrigerant and the type/quantity used will depend on various factors, including the outer packaging selected, initial temperature at time of packing, transit time to consumer and the temperature experienced in transit. The choice made should not be arbitrary but based on sound evidence or advice.

The options include simple ice contained in plastic, frozen gel pads and plastic packs containing a frozen, ready-made eutectic mixture.

Gel pads often come as a sheet of small, plastic fabric sachets, containing a powder that will swell to form a gel when submerged in water. The gel sachets can then be frozen, ready for use. When purchasing such products, care must be taken to ensure they are suitable for use with food.